Causes of Crime

Distinguishing Between Fact and Opinion

Curriculum Consultant: JoAnne Buggey, Ph.D.
College of Education, University of Minnesota

By Stacey L. Tipp

Greenhaven Press, Inc.
Post Office Box 289009
San Diego, CA 92198-9009

Titles in the opposing viewpoints juniors series:

Advertising	Male/Female Roles
AIDS	Nuclear Power
Alcohol	The Palestinian Conflict
Animal Rights	Patriotism
Causes of Crime	Population
Child Abuse	Poverty
Death Penalty	Prisons
Drugs and Sports	Smoking
Endangered Species	Television
The Environment	Toxic Wastes
Garbage	The U.S. Constitution
Gun Control	The War on Drugs
The Homeless	Working Mothers
Immigration	Zoos

Cover photo by: COMSTOCK INC./R. Michael Stuckey

Library of Congress Cataloging-in-Publication Data

Tipp, Stacey L., 1963-
    Causes of Crime : distinguishing between fact and opinion/by
    Stacey L. Tipp ; curriculum consultant, JoAnne Buggey.
        p. cm. — (Opposing viewpoints juniors)
    Summary: Presents opposing viewpoints on the subject of crime and
how it may be affected by poverty, genetics, drug use, and easy
access to guns.
    ISBN 0-89908-615-2
    1. Criminal behavior—Juvenile literature. 2. Criminal behavior,
Prediction of—Juvenile literature. 3. Crime—United States—
juvenile literature. 4. Critical thinking—Juvenile literature.
[1. Crime.] I. Buggey, JoAnne. II. Title. III. Series.
HV6027.T56   1991
364—dc20   91-22123

CONTENTS

An Introduction to
Opposing Viewpoints

When people disagree, it is hard to figure out who is right. You may decide one person is right just because the person is your friend or relative. But this is not a very good reason to agree or disagree with someone. It is better if you try to understand why these people disagree. On what main points do they differ? Read or listen to each person's argument carefully. Separate the facts and opinions that each person presents. Finally, decide which argument best matches what you think. This process, examining an argument without emotion, is part of what critical thinking is all about.

This is not easy. Many things make it hard to understand and form opinions. People's values, ages, and experiences all influence the way they think. This is why learning to read and think critically is an invaluable skill. Opposing Viewpoints Juniors books will help

you learn and practice skills to improve your ability to read critically. By reading opposing views on an issue, you will become familiar with methods people use to attempt to convince you that their point of view is right. And you will learn to separate the authors' opinions from the facts they present.

Each Opposing Viewpoints Juniors book focuses on one critical thinking skill that will help you judge the views presented. Some of these skills are telling fact from opinion, recognizing propaganda techniques, and locating and analyzing the main idea. These skills will allow you to examine opposing viewpoints more easily.

Each viewpoint in this book is paraphrased from the original to make it easier to read. The viewpoints are placed in a running debate and are always placed with the pro view first.

What Is the Difference Between Fact and Opinion?

In this Opposing Viewpoints Juniors book, you will be asked to identify and study statements of fact and statements of opinion. A fact is a statement that can be proved true. Here are some examples of factual statements: "The Statue of Liberty was dedicated in 1886 in New York;" "Dinosaurs are extinct;" and "George Washington was the first U.S. president." It is fairly easy to prove these facts true. For instance, a historian in the year 3000 might need to prove when the Statue of Liberty was dedicated. One way she might do this is to check in the Hall of Records in New York. She would try to find a source such as a newspaper article, the mayor's speech, or a picture of the dedication plaque to verify the date. Sometimes it is harder to check facts. In this book you will be asked to question facts in the viewpoints, and you will be given some ways in which you might go about proving them.

Statements of opinion cannot be proved. An opinion expresses how a person feels about something or what a person thinks is true. Remember the facts we mentioned? They can easily be changed into statements of opinion. For example, "Dinosaurs became extinct because a huge meteor hit the earth," "George Washington was the best president the United States ever had," and "Rebuilding the Statue of Liberty was a waste of money" are all statements of opinion. They express what one person believes to be true.

Opinions are not better than facts. They

are different. Opinions are based on many things, including religious, moral, social, and family values. Opinions can also be based on facts. For instance, many scientists have made intelligent guesses about other planets based on what they know is true about earth. The only way these scientists would know their opinions were right is if they were able to visit other planets and test their guesses. Until their guesses are proved, then, they remain opinions. Some people have opinions that we do not like or with which we disagree. This does not always make their opinions wrong—or right. There is room in our world for many different opinions.

When you read differing views on any issue, it is very important to know when people are using facts and when they are using opinions in an argument. When writers use facts, their arguments are more believable and easier to prove. The more facts the author uses the more the reader can tell that the writer's opinion is based on something other than personal feelings.

Arguments that are based mostly on the author's opinions are impossible to prove factually true. This does not mean these types of arguments are not important. It means that you, as the reader, must decide whether or not you agree or disagree based on personal reasons, not factual ones.

We asked two students to give their opinions on the causes of crime. Examine the following viewpoints. Look for facts and opinions in the arguments.

People commit crimes because they have hard lives.

I think we should feel sorry for criminals. Most criminals are poor and have no families to help them. Also, a lot of criminals were abused as children, or their parents were alcoholics. My friend Jane is a good example. Jane's family is really poor because her parents haven't had jobs in ages. Jane's parents don't pay any attention to her or her little sister, so Jane and her sister are hungry a lot of the time. Last month, Jane was so hungry that she stole some food from a grocery store. She was caught by the store manager who threatened to put her in jail. Instead of threatening Jane with jail, we should help her family so they have enough money to take care of themselves.

People commit crimes because they are bad.

I don't think we should feel sorry for criminals. Criminals are bad people. They don't respect the law. They just do whatever they want to do and take whatever they want to take. Just look at Jim. He's this kid in my class who beats up on the other kids, takes their lunch money, and steals stuff from their lockers. He doesn't have any problems. His parents are really nice, and they have money. His dad is an important lawyer in town. Jim's just a bad kid. He's been suspended from school twice already, and I'm glad about that. I think we should punish people who break the laws. If we punish them, maybe they will think twice before they beat up and steal from people.

ANALYZING THE
SAMPLE VIEWPOINTS

Daisy and Buster have very different opinions about the causes of crime. Both of them use facts and opinions in their arguments.

Daisy:

FACTS

Jane's parents haven't had jobs in ages.

Jane was so hungry that she stole some food from a grocery store.

OPINIONS

I think we should feel sorry for criminals.

We should help Jane's family.

Buster:

FACTS

Jim's dad is an important lawyer in town.

Jim's been suspended from school twice already.

OPINIONS

Criminals are bad people.

Jim's just a bad kid.

In this sample, Daisy and Buster have an equal number of facts and opinions, and they both use examples from their personal experiences to support their arguments. Both Daisy and Buster think they are right about the causes of crime. What conclusions would you come to from this sample? Why?

Think of two facts you know and two opinions you have about what causes crime.

As you continue to read through the viewpoints in this book, keep a tally like the one above to compare to the authors' arguments.

CHAPTER 1

PREFACE: Does Poverty Cause Crime?

Crime is a very serious problem in America today. Of all the rich, Western countries, the United States has the highest rate of violent crime. A violent crime is committed every five seconds in this country.

Many people believe that poverty causes much of the crime in the United States. They argue that when people are unable to earn a decent living and cannot get the necessities of life legally, they are more likely to turn to crime. For example, desperate people may steal or rob to get money for food, rent, clothing, and other needed items.

Other people argue that poor people are no more likely than rich people to commit crimes. They point out that the majority of poor people are honest, law-abiding citizens. In fact, some of these observers believe that crime causes poverty, rather than the other way round. For example, they say that violent crime in America's inner cities drives away many businesses. This takes away the jobs these businesses provide to poor residents of these areas.

The next two viewpoints discuss these issues. As you read them, look for the facts and opinions each presents. Which case is more strongly based on fact?

VIEWPOINT 1   Poverty causes crime

Editor's Note: This viewpoint argues that poverty causes much of the crime in America today. As you read, pay close attention to the facts and opinions used to support this argument.

The statement about the young mother facing the possibility of being thrown onto the streets if she did not pay the rent is a fact.

The statement about the richest 1 percent owning 50 percent of the country's wealth is a fact. To check if it is true, you would have to find out what studies the author is quoting.

Is this statement about respecting society's laws a fact or opinioin? Why?

Of these statements about drug use, which are facts? Which are opinions?

Poverty causes crime. There is no doubt about it. For example, if a young man is poor and hungry, he is much more likely to steal food than if he is rich and well fed. Or if a young mother is poor and she cannot afford to pay the rent, she might steal to get the rent money. After all, if she does not get the money, she and her family could be thrown out of the apartment and onto the streets. On the other hand, if she lived in a nice house that she owned, the thought of stealing money for rent would not even cross her mind. As Mark Green, a lawyer and journalist, wrote in his book *Winning Back America*, "Poverty obviously doesn't excuse crime, but it does just as obviously breed it."

America is a very wealthy country, but the wealth is not shared equally by the American people. Studies show that the richest 1 percent of the people own 50 percent of all the wealth in the country! This inequality makes it really hard to be poor in America. The poor can see that other people—the rich and the middle class—have all the things that the poor people want and need. Poor people see products advertised on television which they will never be able to afford. These include things like fancy cars, big screen TVs, and expensive sneakers. Seeing these things all around them but being unable to afford them makes poor people feel bitter and excluded from society. Because they feel this way, they are less likely to respect society's laws and are more likely to break them.

Poverty also puts a lot of stress on families. When parents work hard and still are barely able to put food on their children's plates, they become frustrated, angry, and depressed. In this condition, they may find it hard to be patient with their children. Sometimes they may even beat or shout at their children. So poverty helps to cause the crime of child abuse.

The stress of poverty also causes many people to use illegal drugs like cocaine and heroin. Poor people use these drugs to escape the sadness and frustration of their everyday lives. These drugs can cause terrible health problems and get the people who use them into trouble with the law. Also, if poor people become addicted to these drugs, they are likely to commit more crimes to

CRIME ROOTS U.S.A.

© Rosen/Rothco. Reprinted with permission.

get the money they need to continue their drug habit.

There has always been a wide gap between the rich and the poor in America, but the gap has grown wider in recent years. Government studies show that the income of poor families with young children dropped by more than 25 percent between 1973 and 1984. Currently, 20 percent of all children in the United States are growing up in poverty. This is a disgrace! The government should do something about this widespread poverty, or crime rates will continue to increase.

Is this final statement a fact or an opinion? Why?

Does poverty cause crime?

What arguments are given in this viewpoint to prove that poverty causes crime? Are these arguments based on fact or opinion?

VIEWPOINT 2 Poverty does not cause crime

Editor's Note: This viewpoint argues that poverty does not cause crime. Instead, it says, crime causes poverty. As you read, note the facts presented.

The notion that poverty causes crime is simply absurd. If it were true, then every resident of every poor neighborhood in America would have a criminal record or be in prison. Obviously this is not the case. Most people who live in poor neighborhoods are law-abiding citizens striving to make better lives for themselves and their families.

If poverty really caused crime, then crime would have been really bad during the Great Depression of the 1930s when most Americans were very poor. Professor Ralph Slovenko points out that this was not true. He states, "During the Great Depression, the

The statement in the opening sentence is the author's opinion. She believes it is true, but there is no way to prove it.

Is Slovenko's statement a fact or opinion? Why?

"REALLY I'M A POOR MAN - EXCEPT FOR THIS GUN
I HAVE NOTHING ELSE IN THE WORLD."

streets, homes, parks, and subways were safe—at a time when college professors sold apples on the street and all Americans were dreadfully deprived. There was no unemployment insurance for the millions of unemployed, and no Social Security."

The truth is that poverty does not cause crime; crime causes poverty! Criminals prey on the poor much more than the rich. The Bureau of Justice, a government agency, states that 9.6 percent of families with yearly incomes of less than $7,500 were burglarized in 1984. This rate was almost twice as high as that for families with yearly incomes between $25,000 and $30,000. The poor are really hurt by burglary. Not only are their possessions stolen, but they usually cannot afford insurance to replace their stolen property. Criminals who prey on the poor make it harder for poor people to climb out of poverty.

Another problem is that the high crime rates in poor inner city neighborhoods have driven away the businesses which could give jobs to residents of those neighborhoods. Crime therefore deprives these residents of the means to escape their poverty. Also, because crime lowers property values in inner city areas, residents who have managed to buy their own homes can only watch helplessly as their property declines in value.

Crime also drains the inner city of its best citizens. Many inner city residents do not want to live there any more because of crime, so they move out. Usually they go to safer neighborhoods at their first opportunity. Unfortunately, the people who leave the inner cities are usually the most educated and skilled. The loss of their positive influence hurts their communities.

In conclusion, poverty does not cause crime; criminals cause crime, and they usually prey on the weakest, poorest members of society. Saying that poverty causes crime puts down honest poor people and neglects the many examples of people who have risen above their poverty by honest means. For instance, Abraham Lincoln was poor, and he became one of America's greatest presidents!

What facts are used to support the view that the poor are most often the victims of crime? Do you find this evidence convincing?

Do the effects of crime on inner city neighborhoods described in these paragraphs convince you that crime causes poverty?

What are the facts and opinions in this paragraph?

Does crime cause poverty?

This viewpoint argues that crime causes poverty. List three facts and three opinions in this viewpoint that support this argument.

Tallying the Facts and Opinions

After reading the two viewpoints on poverty and crime, make a chart similar to the one made for Daisy and Buster on page 8. List the facts and opinions in each viewpoint that support its argument. A chart is started for you below:

Viewpoint 1:

FACTS

The richest 1 percent of the American people own 50 percent of all the wealth in the country.

OPINIONS

If a young man is poor and hungry, he is much more likely to steal food than if he is rich and well fed.

Viewpoint 2:

FACTS

9.6 percent of families with yearly incomes of less than $7,500 were burglarized in 1984.

OPINIONS

The notion that poverty causes crime is simply absurd.

Which viewpoint used more factual statements? Which did you think was the most convincing? Which viewpoint did you personally agree with? Why? List some facts and opinions besides those in the viewpoints that have influenced your opinion.

CHAPTER

PREFACE: Does Genetics
Determine Who
Commits Crime?

Much of our physical appearance, including the color of our eyes and hair, is inherited from our biological parents through our genes. Genes are the material that carry the information about our appearance from our parents' cells to our own before we are born. The word "genetics" means the process by which this information is passed on from generation to generation.

Many people believe that much more than our physical appearance is determined by our genes. They argue that our intelligence, personality, and character are mostly inherited from our parents. Some people say genetics explains why some children develop into criminals and others into law-abiding citizens. If a child's parents are criminals, the chances that the child will also become a criminal are much higher than if the parents were law-abiding. This is because parents who are criminals pass on their own criminal tendencies to the child through their genes. Law-abiding parents pass on their law-abiding tendencies to their children, say the people who hold this view.

Other people do not believe that genetics causes crime. They argue that the way a child is raised determines whether he or she will develop into a criminal. If a child is taught that it is okay to cheat and steal, then it is likely that the child will develop into a dishonest adult. If a child is raised in a violent home, it is likely that the child will develop into a violent adult. These people argue that the environment in which a child is raised is a more important cause of crime than genetics.

The following viewpoints debate whether genetics determines who commits crime.

Editor's Note: In the following viewpoint, the author argues that there is a genetic link to crime. In other words, if a child's parents are criminals, there is a greatly increased chance that the child will also become a criminal.

Genetic factors cause crime. Parents who are criminals pass their own criminal tendencies on to their children through their genes. This is why crime tends to run in families.

Are there any facts in this paragraph?

Other people think that the environment in which children are raised is the real cause of crime. They say that things like poverty, child abuse, racism, and poor education are the main reasons children go on to commit crimes later in their lives. This is a silly argument. Visit any state prison and you will see that it is full of criminals whose parents occupied it twenty years ago.

Do you think that Mednick's method of studying adopted boys is a good way to test the genetic link to crime? Why or why not?

Important scientific studies prove that bad parents have bad kids. One of the most important of these studies was done in Denmark by the famous psychologist Sarnoff Mednick. Mednick's study focused on a group of adopted boys, some of whose natural parents had been criminals. Mednick found that the adopted children whose natural parents were criminals were much more likely to become criminals themselves than adopted boys whose natural parents were not criminals. He also found that boys whose natural parents were criminals were more likely to commit crimes than boys whose adoptive parents were criminals! In other words,

"Which are you—a victim of society or a crook?"

Drawing by Ed Arno; © 1979 The New Yorker Magazine, Inc.

genetics, not environment, is the best guide to whether a child will later become a criminal.

In another study, Raymond Crowe of the University of Iowa followed the progress of forty-six adopted children who had been born to women prisoners. Crowe found that six of these children had anti-social personality disorders. Only one of a similar group of adoptees born to non-criminal mothers had similar disorders.

This is an important finding because such disorders cause people to commit anti-social actions. These actions include lying, stealing, and crimes of violence. While anti-social personality disorders can be mild, in their worst forms they are found in killers like Ted Bundy, who murdered more than thirty women.

We cannot ignore these scientific studies which prove the genetic link to crime. With more research in this area, we may be able to use our knowledge to prevent criminal behavior before it starts. We could identify young offenders and give them psychological and educational counseling. We could help young offenders develop into law-abiding citizens, not criminals.

How convincing do you find Crowe's study?

Do you agree that counseling could prevent young offenders from developing into criminals?

Does genetics cause crime?

How did the author's use of fact and opinion affect your evaluation of this viewpoint? Why?

The tendency to commit crime is not genetic

Editor's Note: The author of this viewpoint argues that the environment in which a child is raised determines whether he or she will become a criminal. Consider the evidence the author supplies. Is it based on fact or opinion?

Are there more facts or more opinions in this paragraph?

There is very little evidence to prove that genetic factors cause crime. The real causes of crime are environmental. In other words, the more a young child is exposed to such negative factors as poverty, child abuse, alcoholism, drug abuse, and racism, the more likely it is that he or she will become involved in crime. David L. Bazelon, a respected judge and expert on psychiatry, states, "The roots of street crime lie in poverty *plus*—prejudice, plus poor housing, plus inadequate education, plus insufficient food and medical care, and perhaps most importantly, plus a bad family environment or no family at all."

One of the most harmful environmental factors is physical and

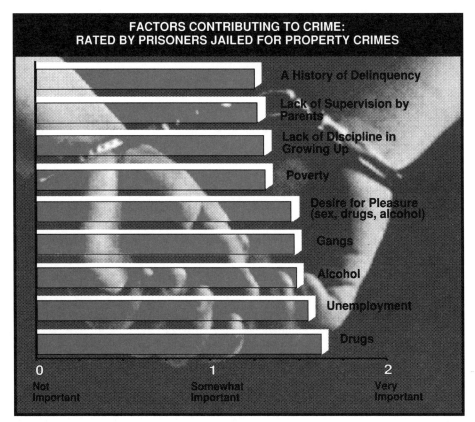

FACTORS CONTRIBUTING TO CRIME: RATED BY PRISONERS JAILED FOR PROPERTY CRIMES

A History of Delinquency

Lack of Supervision by Parents

Lack of Discipline in Growing Up

Poverty

Desire for Pleasure (sex, drugs, alcohol)

Gangs

Alcohol

Unemployment

Drugs

| 0 | 1 | 2 |
| Not Important | Somewhat Important | Very Important |

Source: Figgie International, Inc., *The Figgie Report Part VI - The Business of Crime: The Criminal Perspective*, 1988.

sexual abuse of children. Studies estimate that 33 percent of adults who were abused as children become child abusers when they grow up. They do not carry a gene that makes them commit this crime. Rather, the *experience* of suffering abuse and violence causes them to inflict the same treatment on others.

To abused children, violence becomes so much a normal part of life that they often go on to commit violent crimes when they grow up. Consider the case of Charles Manson, the famous murderer who is in prison for a 1969 killing spree which left seven people dead. Manson had a horrible childhood. It is largely responsible for his long and violent criminal career.

Manson was born in 1934 in Cincinnati, Ohio, to an unmarried fifteen-year-old girl. No one really wanted him, and he was shuttled about to many different homes until the age of twelve, when his mother asked the Indiana state authorities to take care of him. Since that time, Manson has spent most of his life behind bars, in reform school, training school, jail, and prison.

Manson has written and and spoken a great deal about his unhappy childhood. He rightly blames his behavior on the fact that he was neglected and abused as a little boy. In Manson's words, "Hey, listen, by the time I was old enough to think or remember, I had been shoved around and left with people who were strangers, even to those I knew. Rejection, more than love and acceptance, has been a part of my life since birth."

Because violent crime is caused by bad influences on our children, we must do all we can to remove these influences from our children's lives. We must eliminate child abuse, poverty, drug abuse, racism, and other negative environmental influences. This is the only way to make children's lives better and to ensure that they will not become criminals.

We must firmly reject the outdated and false genetic theory of crime. As Andrew Vachss, a well-known supporter of children's rights, puts it, "Criminals are made, not born—there is no biogenetic code that produces a violent rapist, a child molester, or a serial killer."

Do you agree with the opinions expressed in this paragraph? Why or why not?

Do you agree that an unhappy childhood, like Manson's, could turn a person into a killer?

Is this quotation a fact or opinion? Why?

Genetics or environment?

This viewpoint argues that a bad environment can determine whether a child grows up to be a criminal.
After reading both viewpoints, do you believe that genetics or environment is a more important cause of crime? Why?

Distinguishing Between Fact and Opinion

The following sentences are based on information contained in the readings. Write *F* beside any statement you believe is fact, or something that can be proven to be true. Mark *O* beside any statement you believe is an opinion, or what one person believes to be true.

EXAMPLE: Sarnoff Mednick is a scientist who has studied the link between genetics and crime.

ANSWER: Fact: This statement could be proven by calling the library and asking the librarian for a list of Mednick's books and articles.

Answer

1. Bad parents have bad kids. _____

2. Raymond Crowe's study found that six out of forty-six adopted children born to criminal mothers had anti-social personality disorders. _____

3. Ted Bundy was a famous killer who murdered more than thirty women. _____

4. Counseling is the only way to prevent young offenders from developing into criminals. _____

5. Studies show that one-third of people who were abused as children become child abusers when they grow up. _____

6. Charles Manson is not to blame for the murders he committed; his horrible childhood is to blame. _____

7. Charles Manson was born in 1934 in Cincinnati, Ohio, to an unmarried fifteen-year-old girl. _____

8. Removing negative environmental influences from our children's lives is the only way to stop them from becoming criminals. _____

CHAPTER 3

PREFACE: Does the Use of Illegal Drugs Cause Crime?

There is widespread concern in America today about illegal drugs such as crack cocaine and heroin. These drugs affect all segments of American society and cause many serious problems, including, some say, an appalling number of violent crimes.

Many people argue that drug use itself affects people's behavior, causing them to commit acts of violence. They further argue that drug users commit an enormous number of crimes to get the money needed to continue their drug use. These crimes include robbery, prostitution, and murder. Finally, the drug trade is a major source of violent crime. The participants establish gangs, fight over turf, and exact terrible retributions against those who cross them.

Others disagree about the connection between drugs and crime. They say there is no evidence that drugs make people commit crimes. Instead, they blame anti-drug *laws* for the increase in violent crime. They say that if drugs like cocaine and heroin were available legally, there would be much less drug-related crime in America. The government would regulate the drug industry. It would cut out the dealers and pushers who are the source of so much drug-related crime. The government could also set low drug prices so that addicts would no longer be forced to commit crimes to afford their drugs. Most of these observers also believe the government should provide drug treatment programs to wean addicts off dangerous drugs.

The following two viewpoints present opposing arguments on the link between illegal drug use and crime. When reading these viewpoints, pay attention to the authors' uses of fact and opinion.

Editor's Note: The following viewpoint argues that drug use is responsible for much of the violent crime in America. Pay attention to the facts and opinions used to support this argument.

How many facts are in this opening paragraph? How many opinions?

What facts are used to support the view that illegal drugs cause crime? How convincing do you find them?

Is this statement about users doing anything for a fix a fact or opinion? Do you agree with the statement?

Drugs are very dangerous substances. People should avoid them at all costs. They are responsible for the crime wave of the 1980s and 1990s. Statistics from all over the country prove this. For example, police officers in Chattanooga, Tennessee, are attempting to cope with huge increases in crime caused by crack users. The police say that at least two out of every three robbery suspects is a drug user. The users prefer to rob convenience stores and fast-food restaurants because they are easy targets. The police say that the majority of these thieves simply need money to get high.

Studies show that illegal drugs alter people's moods and encourage them to commit crimes. For instance, a 1988 study of child-abuse deaths in Philadelphia found that 50 percent of these deaths were caused by parents who used cocaine. Also, according to the Department of Justice, more than 80 percent of criminals arrested for violent crimes (including rape, murder, and assault) were on drugs at the time they committed their crimes.

With some illegal drugs like heroin and cocaine, the drug users need increasing amounts of the drug as their addiction worsens. Consuming such large amounts of drugs can be very expensive, but price does not deter the addict. Users will do *anything* for their fix. They will beg, steal, rob, and even have sex with strangers in exchange for drugs. And, of course, drug users will kill to get their drugs. Two cases from New York prove this point beyond any doubt. In 1988, a sixteen-year-old boy murdered a young man in Brooklyn, taking two hundred dollars to buy crack. In that same year, another New York crack user killed five people in eight days to get money to buy crack.

Unfortunately, these cases are only the tip of the iceberg. The Federal Bureau of Investigation estimates that 1,600 people are murdered each year in drug-related street crimes. These figures do not take into account the hundreds of people killed each year in shoot-outs between criminals who supply drugs to users. Often, the victims are innocent bystanders who happened to be in the wrong place at the wrong time.

Vernia Brown was one of these victims. Vernia was a nineteen-

Percentage of Male Arrestees Testing Positive For Any Drug
(June-November 1987)

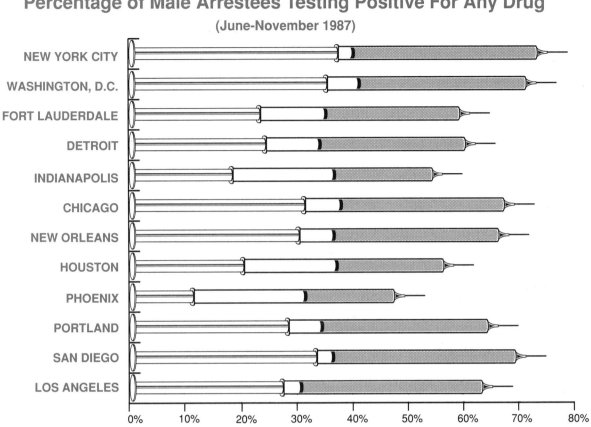

Source: United States Government Printing Office.

year-old resident of Bronx, New York. She was killed by stray bullets from a gun battle over illegal drugs in March 1988. She was an innocent young woman and not involved in the argument in any way.

Drug use is responsible for the huge increases in violent crime in recent years. If we want to reduce crime and make our streets safe once again, we should not take drugs, and we should severely punish those who do. "Just Saying No" is a good place to start.

Does the crime described in this paragraph convince you that drug use causes crime?

Are there any facts in this paragraph?

Just Say No

The author believes we should say no to drugs and punish people who do use drugs. Do you think that this strategy is enough to reduce the number of crimes committed by drug users? Why or Why not?

Are there any facts in this opening statement?

How many opinions can you count in this paragraph?

Drug use is not the cause of the crime wave of recent years. Rather, increased crime is caused by the *laws* which make drugs like heroin and cocaine illegal. Many important people believe this.

The fact is that people who use cocaine or other illegal drugs do not immediately go crazy and start murdering people or committing other violent crimes. Indeed, studies have shown that it is very rare for drugs to cause someone to commit a violent act. However, it is true that drug users are forced to commit crimes to get the money they need to pay for expensive drugs. Why are drugs expensive? The answer is because they are illegal.

Basically, those criminals who sell illegal drugs demand large

Annual Deaths in the U.S. Caused by Drug Laws

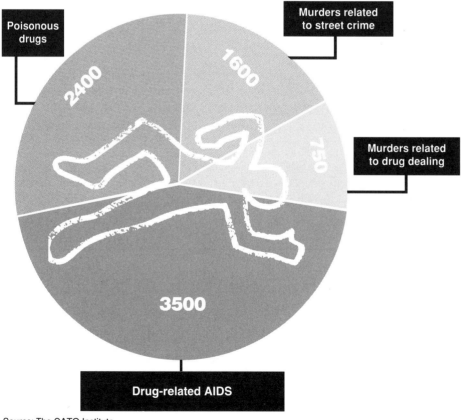

Poisonous drugs — 2400

Murders related to street crime — 1600

Murders related to drug dealing — 750

Drug-related AIDS — 3500

Source: The CATO Institute.

profits to make breaking the drug laws worth their while. After all, if they are caught, they could be sent to prison for a long time. Because drug dealers sell drugs at very high prices, addicts are forced to commit crimes like robbery, burglary, and prostitution to get the large amounts of money needed to buy their drugs. David Boaz is a researcher at the CATO Institute, an organization that reports on economic issues, located in Washington, D.C. Boaz estimates that each drug addict in the nation's capital steals an average of $600 worth of goods per day to feed his or her drug habit!

Because the illegal drug business is so profitable, drug dealers are willing to do just about anything to protect and increase their profits. This includes threatening, bullying, and even killing people. Huge drug profits are the real cause of the street violence in cities like New York, Los Angeles, and Washington, D.C.

In 1987, the New York City Police Department announced that 38 percent of murders in the city were drug-related. However, Deputy Chief of Police Raymond W. Kelly pointed out that these murders were not caused by crazed drug addicts, but by drug dealers arguing over the division of drug profits. As Mr. Kelly put it, "When we say drug-related, we're essentially talking about territorial disputes or disputes over possession. . . . We're not talking about where somebody is deranged because they're on a drug."

Does the evidence from the New York City Police Department convince you that drug laws cause crime?

How can we reduce drug-related crime? The best answer is to make drugs legal. If we legalize drugs, the government would take over the industry. It would regulate the price and quality of the different drugs. The government could make drugs so inexpensive that addicts would not have to steal or commit other crimes to obtain their drugs. Also, if the government controlled the drug trade, the drug pushers would be cut out of the business and would not have any more profits to fight over.

How would you feel if the government got involved in the drug business? Why?

Of course, the government should also do everything in its power to get people off drugs. It should provide them with treatment and counseling programs. In time, drug addiction and the violence of the drug trade would decline and die.

Is this conclusion a fact or opinion? Why?

Should we make drugs legal?

The author believes that legalizing drugs will greatly reduce drug-related crime. Do you agree? Do you think that more people would be tempted to try drugs if they were available legally?

3 Understanding Editorial Cartoons

Throughout this book you have seen cartoons that illustrate the ideas in the viewpoints. Editorial cartoons are an effective and usually humorous way of presenting an opinion on an issue. While many cartoons are easy to understand, others, like the one below, may require more thought. The cartoon below deals with the connection between drug use and violent crime. It is similar to the cartoons that appear in your daily newspaper.

   Look at the cartoon. Do you think the cartoonist believes that drug use causes crime? Why or why not? Do you agree with the cartoonist? Why or why not?

Bob Dix, *The Union Leader*. Reprinted with permission.

CHAPTER 4

PREFACE: Does Easy Access to Guns Cause Crime?

Gun control is one of the most hotly debated issues in America. One of the many disagreements in the gun control debate is whether the widespread availability of guns causes crime.

Many people believe that easy access to guns is at least partly responsible for rising crime rates in the United States. They argue that if laws restricted people's access to guns, crime rates would fall. Gun control supporters believe these laws would prevent incidents like the shooting death of John Lennon and the attempted assassination of former president Ronald Reagan. They also believe that other violent crimes, particularly the large numbers of murders caused by family disputes, would be reduced if gun control laws were passed.

However, many people do not agree that stricter controls on guns would reduce crime. These opponents of gun control laws argue that ordinary citizens need guns to protect themselves against violent criminals. Because gun control laws would leave law-abiding citizens unable to defend themselves, these laws would actually cause crime rates to increase, gun supporters say.

The viewpoints in this chapter debate whether easy access to guns causes crime.

Editor's Note: The following viewpoint argues that easy access to guns causes crime. The author believes that controlling access to guns will reduce crime.

How many facts are in this opening paragraph? How many opinions?

Anyone can get a gun in America. It is as easy as pie! Unfortunately, the widespread availability of guns causes a huge number of crimes in this country. Consider murder as an example. In 1987, 20,100 Americans were murdered. One estimate is that approximately 60 percent of these victims were killed with firearms!

Does the evidence presented in this paragraph convince you that easy access to guns causes murder?

Easy access to guns has caused the violent deaths of some of America's top leaders. They include John F. Kennedy, Robert Kennedy, and Martin Luther King, Jr. Other leaders have only narrowly escaped death from guns. Former president Ronald Reagan managed to cheat death on March 30, 1981, when John Hinkley tried to murder him. Fortunately, Reagan was not seriously wounded. His press secretary James Brady was not so lucky. Brady was shot in the head by Hinkley. He has been confined to a wheelchair ever since, and he suffers constant pain. James Brady and his wife, Sarah, have been very strong supporters of gun control ever since 1981. Sarah Brady expresses outrage at the ease with which Hinkley got the gun which shot her husband. "I ask why it is possible for the John Hinkleys of this world to walk into a store, buy a handgun, and go out and shoot people," she says. "He [Hinkley] walked into a Dallas pawnshop, purchased a cheap Saturday night special—no questions asked."

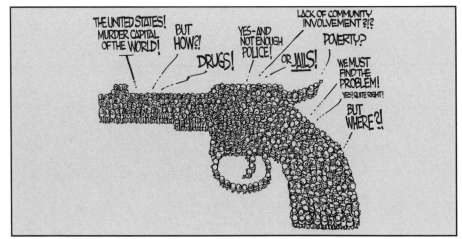

Reprinted with special permission of King Features Syndicate, Inc.

Gun murders are not just committed by weirdos like John Hinkley though. Many murders are so-called "crimes of passion." These include family squabbles and arguments between lovers, friends, or drinking buddies. If guns were not around, many of these disputes would not end in death. Studies estimate that approximately 60 percent of murders are crimes of passion. Irvin Block is an advocate of stricter gun control. He states, "Murder is usually a spontaneous outburst of unreasoning rage in which the murderer goes for the most readily available weapon. Given a choice, the potential murderer is likely to reach for a pistol if one is available. . . . [The handgun] is the most efficient weapon for murder at close range between people who know one another."

Other rich, Western countries have much stricter gun control laws than America does. As a result, they have many fewer gun deaths. For example, Great Britain has very strict gun laws. Anyone who wants a gun in Great Britain has to get a certificate from the police. A person can only get a certificate if he or she has a good reason, such as being a member of a hunting or gun club. People who are found to have a gun without a certificate are harshly punished. As a result of these strict laws, in 1985 Britain had only one death caused by a handgun for every one thousand such deaths in America. We simply must get tighter gun laws in this country!

Guns are not only used to kill people though. They are used to commit robberies, kidnappings, rapes, muggings, and all other sorts of crimes. Criminals are cowards. Guns allow them to commit crimes they would otherwise be too scared to commit. As Irvin Block writes, handguns can "be concealed and used with surprise effect which makes them the prime tool of the criminal. They are personal, close-range weapons, an extension of the owner's aggressions or fears. With a flick of the wrist, a handgun—'the great equalizer'—can make a big man out of a small one." In 1987, there were 91,100 reported rapes, 517,700 robberies, and 855,090 aggravated assaults. If guns were not available, it is certain these numbers would be much, much, lower.

Is Block's statement a fact or opinion? Why?

Does the example of Great Britain convince you that America needs to control access to guns?

Is this conclusion a fact or opinion? Why?

Does easy access to guns cause crime?

How did the author's use of fact and opinion affect your evaluation of this viewpoint? Why?

Easy access to guns does not cause crime

Editor's Note: The following viewpoint argues that easy access to guns actually reduces crime, not causes it.

How many opinions can you count in this opening paragraph?

Guns do not cause crime. Criminals cause crime! We must fight attempts to limit people's access to guns. If laws restrict access to guns, the only people left with guns will be criminals. This is because only law-abiding people will obey gun control laws. Criminals will continue to get their guns the way they always have—by stealing guns or buying them on the black market. If gun control laws were enacted, law-abiding citizens would have no means to defend themselves against armed, dangerous criminals. They would be sitting ducks!

It is a fact that guns reduce crime. Many examples prove this point. In February 1991, Theresa Paulfranz of Chesapeake, Virginia, was punched by an acquaintance who threatened to rape her. Theresa's neighbor made the assailant leave, but he later returned and kicked in the door to her home. He again threatened her. Theresa fired a single shot from her .38 caliber revolver, killing her attacker. In the same month, James Militello of Sun Valley,

'HEY, MA! GET ME ONE OF THE KID'S PEASHOOTERS, HERE COME SOME THUGS!'

U.S. STATISTICS SHOW 169,000 MACHINE GUNS ARE NOW BEING USED AND ARE COMMONDLACE IN ROBBERIES.

THE UNARMED CITIZEN

NOW THEY'VE GOT MACHINE GUNS!

Dobbins. *The Union Leader.* Reprinted with permission.

Nevada, was driving home from a shooting trip. He saw two men violently beating a third man at an intersection. James picked up his unloaded .22 and went to the rescue. He forced the two men to leave and took the injured man to the hospital. Finally, in January 1991 in Flint, Michigan, an armed robber demanded money from a storeowner. He got the money and fled, but was chased by two employees with a gun kept in the store. The police came and found the two employees sitting on the criminal, caught after a two-block chase.

These are individual examples of criminals who were thwarted because their victims had guns. However, there are also many surveys and statistics which show that guns reduce crime. In the 1960s, police in Orlando, Florida, trained 2,500 women to use handguns after a series of rapes. After one year, the rape total had fallen by 88 percent and aggravated assault and burglary dropped by 25 percent. Also, between 1979 and 1985, the National Crime Survey conducted a study on the crime of robbery. The study found that when a robbery victim resists with a gun, the robbery success rate is only 30 percent and the victim injury rate is 17 percent. In contrast, when the robbery victim does not resist with a gun, the robber succeeds 88 percent of the time, and the victim is injured 25 percent of the time!

All these examples and statistics prove that guns are necessary for self-defense against violent crime. Restricting people's access to guns will only benefit criminals. As David B. Kopel, a former assistant district attorney in Manhattan, New York, argues, "Guns reduce crime; gun control causes crime."

Do the examples and studies presented in these paragraphs convince you that guns reduce crime? Why or why not?

Is Kopel's statement a fact or an opinion? Why?

Does easy access to guns cause or reduce crime?

This viewpoint argues that restricting access to guns will increase crime. Why? After reading both viewpoints, do you believe we should restrict people's access to guns? Why or why not?

Five topics are listed below. Choose one of them and write two paragraphs about it. Use facts in paragraph one and opinions in paragraph two.

Afterwards, share your paragraphs with two other people. Ask them which paragraph is more effective. Why?

1. Restricting access to guns will reduce crime.
2. Criminals cause crime.
3. Law-abiding citizens need guns to protect themselves from criminals.
4. Great Britain has few gun deaths because of its strict gun control laws.
5. Guns reduce crime.

Sample paragraphs

Topic: Guns have killed or wounded many of America's top leaders and should therefore be restricted or banned.

PARAGRAPH 1:

FACTS

Guns have killed many of America's top leaders. America's slain leaders include former president John F. Kennedy, his brother Robert, and civil rights leader Martin Luther King Jr. Other leaders have been wounded by guns. Former president Ronald Reagan was shot in the chest by John Hinkley in 1981. Hinkley purchased the gun at a pawnshop in Dallas, and very few questions were asked. These crimes have made many Americans question the ease with which people like Hinkley can obtain weapons. While some Americans advocate restricting access to guns, others support a complete weapons ban.

PARAGRAPH 2:

OPINIONS

Guns have killed many of America's top leaders. Men like John F. Kennedy were cut down in their prime by criminals who wanted to get their faces on television and in the newspapers. Leaders do not get killed in other countries where guns are not so available. We must either restrict or completely ban guns or another of our leaders will probably be killed soon. We must protect our leaders or this country will fall apart.